Original title:
Forest Feels and Fables

Copyright © 2025 Creative Arts Management OÜ
All rights reserved.

Author: Lila Davenport
ISBN HARDBACK: 978-1-80567-176-3
ISBN PAPERBACK: 978-1-80567-475-7

Shadows Dance in Emerald Light

In the woods where shadows play,
The squirrels gossip all the day.
A raccoon juggles shiny finds,
While a snail stirs, dreaming of climbs.

The trees whisper jokes in greenting tones,
As chirps and chuckles fill the thrones.
Little mushrooms giggle in rows,
While a fox tap-dances on his toes.

Beneath the Boughs of Time

Under branches, time takes a pause,
Where the owl hoots out loud 'give me applause!'
The turtles debate who is more slow,
While a shy deer peeks from below.

The old oak claims it knows it all,
But the young sprouts just laugh and sprawl.
A raccoon pulls pranks like a fabled king,
Every twig caught up in his mischievous fling.

The Heartbeat of the Wild

With every thump, the wild heart sings,
A playful breeze flits by on wings.
The ants throw a picnic, all in a line,
While the foxes join for a comical dine.

A rabbit tells tales, both tall and wide,
While the bees buzz in laughter, filling with pride.
The woodpecker drums a song with flair,
In a rhythm so silly, it twirls through the air.

Guardians of the Green

The guardians peek from their leafy lairs,
Spying on wanderers with playful stares.
A wise old toad offers some junk,
While giggling fairies think it's all bunk.

The hedgehogs roll in a pie of leaves,
While the badgers weave mischievous thieves.
With every rustle, their laughter resounds,
In this realm where joy endlessly pounds.

The Enchantment of Evergreen

Under leaves that laugh and sway,
A squirrel sings without delay.
He juggles acorns round and round,
While sleepy bears snooze on the ground.

A rabbit tells a tall, grand tale,
Of moonlit nights and dancing snail.
The trees nod softly, wise and green,
In this merry woodland scene.

Treasures Lost in Timber

A raccoon found a shiny shoe,
He thought it was a treasure, too!
But when he tried to wear it tight,
He tripped and caused a funny fright.

A chipmunk claims he lost his hat,
It's hiding where the wild things chat.
But every time he's close, it flees,
With laughter carried on the breeze.

Shaded Stories of the Wild

The wise old owl tells jokes at night,
With punchlines that take flight.
The deer chuckle, prancing about,
As fireflies dance and flit about.

A fox brings snacks of berries sweet,
While raccoons wiggle their little feet.
"Who steals my snack?" the fox cries loud,
But all that's left is just a crowd.

The Canvas of Chrysanthemums

In the garden where blooms collide,
A snail with paintbrush takes his stride.
He's color-blind but full of glee,
Says, "All art's great, just wait and see!"

The daisies giggle, turning pink,
As bees just buzz and never think.
They join the fun, pollinate the day,
With stories told in buzzing play.

The Call of the Cedar

In the shade where squirrels play,
A cedar calls, come what may.
With a bark that bears a grin,
It whispers secrets to the wind.

A chipmunk chuckles, tails a-flare,
Telling tales of chairs to share.
Acorns tumble, a nutty plan,
The tree just rolls its woody span.

Wandering Through Whispers

Beneath the boughs, the breeze does prance,
Leaves laugh like they're in a dance.
The shadows play hide-and-seek,
While crickets sing a silly beat.

A mushroom wears a polka-dot hat,
In a debate with a chatty cat.
Their banter echoes, quite absurd,
Across the stage of green, unheard.

Sylphs and Spirits of the Thicket

Sprites and shadows play a key,
In the thicket, wild and free.
They giggle 'neath the twilight glow,
As raccoons tango in a row.

A hare is dressed in leafy threads,
Holding court, while owl just treads.
The night ignites with their delight,
While fireflies blink, their disco light.

Reflections on a Leafy Canvas

On a canvas made of leaves,
A painter squirrel quietly weaves.
His brush—a twig; his palette—mud,
He splatters joy with joyful thud.

Behind him, bushes cluck and cheer,
Each stroke incites a crazy deer.
With giggles high and details low,
Nature's art becomes a show.

The Riddle of the Rushing Stream

A bubbling brook began to sing,
Telling tales of a slippery thing.
What swims with glee, yet wears no shoes?
A fish with flair, that loves to cruise.

The water giggles as it flows fast,
While pebbles gossip of legends past.
With every splash, the secrets teem,
Oh, what a sight, this watery dream!

A Tantalizing Tangle of Twigs

Twists and turns in a playful maze,
Where branches whisper in sunny rays.
A squirrel darts, with a nut in tow,
While hidden rabbits put on a show.

What's that sound? A wind-blown tune!
Is it a song from a magical loon?
Nests of laughter in the trees do sway,
In this quirky grove, we dance and play.

The Magic Beneath the Multitude

Beneath the leaves where shadows dwell,
Tiny creatures weave their spell.
A beetle dons a hat so bright,
While fireflies spark the fading light.

With a hop and skip, a show unfolds,
A mischief of mice, brave and bold.
They twirl and cheer, a jolly lot,
In this vibrant world, they share the spot.

Relics of the Resilient Roots

Roots twist deep, a tangled tale,
Where stories linger and laughter sails.
An old tree grins, its bark like skin,
With wisdom to share, let the fun begin!

Who knows what quirks hide in the ground?
A gnome with jokes might just be found.
With a wink and nod, he spins a yarn,
Of whimsical deeds on a grassy lawn.

The Kiss of the Morning Dew

In the dawn, when the critters yawn,
A droplet slips from the leaves at dawn.
The grass shimmies, it giggles bright,
As ants wear hats, ready for their flight.

A butterfly winks, then does a twirl,
While a snail checks its speed – such a whirl!
They burst into laughter, take to the sky,
"Who knew morning dew could cause such a spy?"

Roaming the Roots of Reverie

Beneath the boughs, where shadows dance,
A squirrel jokes, "Should I wear pants?"
The mushrooms chuckle, the ferns all sway,
As giggles echo through the leafy ballet.

A fox tells tales of witty dreams,
While the lizards plot out their laser beams.
"Catch me if you can!" they yell out loud,
While a crow caws, "You're not that proud!"

Beyond the Bramble: A Tale

Through thorny paths, the raccoons creep,
With tangled tales and secrets they keep.
A bear in a hat, oh what a sight,
He shares silly puns under the moonlight.

The brambles hum a tune so sweet,
While a hedgehog nods to each funky beat.
A little mouse rolls in laughter's embrace,
"Do these shoes make my feet look like ace?"

The Heart of the Hidden Hollow

In a nook where the chatter is brisk and loud,
A chipmunk claims he's a stand-up proud.
His jokes fly high, like fireflies at night,
As laughter rings, glowing warm and bright.

A wise old owl hoots a puzzled rhyme,
"Why did the branch take a break from the climb?"
With giggles shared by critters all around,
In this secret glen, joy is truly found.

Petals on the Forest Floor

The flowers giggle in the breeze,
Their colors dance like playful seas.
A dandelion dons a lion's mane,
While bees wear crowns, but feel no strain.

A snail slides by with royal grace,
Sporting a shell, a slow-paced race.
"Hey, watch me glow!" a firefly winks,
As mushrooms chat and share their drinks.

Symphony of the Spruce

The trees are strumming on their limbs,
With squirrels tapping on some whims.
A woodpecker plays a peppy beat,
While acorns bounce, a tasty treat.

A loony owl hoots a crazy tune,
As hedgehogs waddle under the moon.
The orchestra plays, a merry cheer,
While raccoons juggle, drawing near.

Glimmers of Gold and Green

A sunbeam tickles the leaves so bright,
While frogs croak songs, a silly sight.
In a puddle, a pretty frog sings,
"I'm the king of the swamps, behold my rings!"

Ladybugs strut in ballet attire,
While crickets chirp like a funky choir.
A butterfly flops with a clumsy flair,
Spreading joy everywhere it dares.

Mysteries Under the Canopy

The shadows whisper, a cheeky plot,
As raccoons giggle in the distracted spot.
A mischievous fox with a polished grin,
Steals a hat where the forest begins.

A wise old turtle tells a tall tale,
Of snaggle-toothed fish and a wingless whale.
The fables twist and twirl a little,
As the critters laugh, oh, what a riddle!

Songs of Springtime and Shadows

Giggling leaves dance on the breeze,
A squirrel slips, oh what a tease!
Chasing tails in a sunny plight,
While birds gossip from morning to night.

The sun wears a hat made of rays,
In patches bright, where the rabbit plays.
A toad croaks a tune, quite a show,
As ants march in line, moving slow.

Bees buzz jokes in floral debates,
While a fox tips his hat, maybe waits.
Chirping crickets, the night's own jest,
Stumble on laughs, it's all for the best.

With shadows that stretch and then grin,
They tease the day, coaxing a spin.
Life in the green is a humorous play,
Where laughter lives in each sunny ray.

The Pageantry of Pine Needles

Among the pines in a tangled twist,
A crow tells tales that can't be missed.
With needle crowns and acorn caps,
They waltz around in hilarious laps.

The stoic trees wear coats of green,
While critters wear shoes that are quite unseen.
A chipmunk struts with an air quite grand,
Declares himself king of the woodland band.

Pine cones tumble with comic flair,
As wobbly squirrels dart here and there.
The sun peeks in, giving a grin,
Adding warmth to the chaos within.

Laughter echoes in this prickly realm,
Where the tallest trees take the helm.
They sway with joy, a merry incline,
In the pageantry of the woodland divine.

Echoes of the Emerald Expanse

In the green expanse where giggles roam,
Bunnies hop home, calling it their dome.
A turtle chuckles, slow but sly,
While wise old owls just wink and fly.

Mossy carpets invite you to play,
As vibrant flowers boast their bouquet.
A chattering stream hums a tune,
While shadows dance under the moon.

Nutty narratives, a hedgehog's glee,
With wisecracks shared 'neath the old oak tree.
A ladybug lands, spins a yarn,
Of flower parties from dusk till dawn.

Lively echoes of nature's jest,
Wrap the wanderer in a cozy nest.
In vibrant whispers, joy we find,
Where laughter and antics intertwine.

Secrets of the Sylvan Shade

In the grove stood a squirrel with flair,
He challenged a rabbit to twirl in midair.
The rabbit tripped once and fell on a log,
The squirrel just laughed, and then danced like a frog.

Mushrooms conspired in colors so bright,
They whispered sweet secrets all through the night.
A hedgehog bustled with riddle and rhyme,
While fireflies giggled, just wasting their time.

The Heartbeat of Ancient Trees

A wise old oak wore a crown made of leaves,
He told all the young ones, "Now here's what he weaves!"

"Don't argue with the wind or get lost in your bark,
You'll get swirled around, and that's not quite smart!"

A chipmunk chimed in with a song that was silly,
He did a quick jig that was rather quite frilly.
The trees chuckled deeply as branches would sway,
While nature's own choir just played all day.

Tales Woven in Moss

A patch of green giggled beneath a great stone,
"I'm the softest of beds, you can't say I'm prone!"
A snail slid on over, thinking it grand,
Then tripped on a twig—oh, wasn't life planned?

The ferns whispered gossip of love in the gloom,
While light through the branches did dance and consume.
A toad croaked a tale – of a prince and his hat,
But no one believed him; they laughed just at that.

Moonlight on Leafy Lanes

Under the moon, a band of wise owls,
Held meetings about raucous, unruly night prowls.
They hooted and hollered, then played peek-a-boo,
Which startled a raccoon, who screamed, "Who are you?"

With shadows and giggles, the night dived in cheer,
As critters convened, they released all their fear.
The night would unfold, with pranks on the rise,
While echoing laughter lit up the night skies.

Beneath the Bowery of Dreams.

Underneath a crooked tree,
A squirrel wearing shades did see,
A rabbit in a sunlit hat,
Dancing with a playful cat.

The owl hooted tunes so weird,
While hedgehogs in a band appeared,
They strummed on leaves, a leafy song,
In this wild world where dreams belong.

A raccoon with a wink so sly,
Juggled acorns as they fly,
Ducklings quacked in rhythmic time,
A symphony, oh, so sublime!

As twilight painted skies in gold,
The critters crooned their tales so bold,
In laughter shared beneath the stars,
Funny fables, near and far.

Whispers of the Woodlands

A fox with socks danced on a log,
While frogs joined in, a boisterous cog,
The tales of trees swayed to the beat,
   As beetles tapped their tiny feet.

Mice in capes played hide and seek,
While antlers twirled, a sight unique,
And whispers curled like smoke in air,
   Bringing giggles everywhere!

A wobbly deer attempted ballet,
Stumbling, tumbling, in quite a display,
The wildflowers chuckled with glee,
   Nature's jesters, wild and free.

As stars twinkled with a cheeky grin,
The night concluded, let laughter spin,
In whimsical whispers, dreams entwined,
Where joy through the woods can be defined.

Echoes Beneath the Canopy

In the shade where shadows prance,
A giraffe tried the chicken dance,
With cycles slow, it turned about,
While monkeys hollered, dancing out.

A porcupine in a polka-dot,
Thought he could be a famous tot,
But with each jump, he'd poke a friend,
And so the dance would soon suspend.

A chameleon dressed in bright confetti,
Changed its hues, oh, wasn't that petty?
It giggled as the colors played,
In a comedy show, nature displayed.

The echoes of laughter soared up high,
As critters paused, and none were shy,
In the canopy's embrace so wide,
Unfolding chuckles, side by side.

Embracing the Emerald

A snail in shades was quite a sight,
Racing with slugs in the morning light,
Each one said, "I'm fast, you see!"
But who could tell? They all drank tea!

A toad in a vest was singing loud,
With dragonflies forming a crowd,
They tapped their wings in rhythm neat,
While ants formed lines to groove their feet.

A bear in boots tried cooking stew,
But spilled the pot! Oh, what a view,
With giggles bubbling, stories spread,
As veggies danced and berries fled!

Through emerald fields, fun to behold,
Jokes lush and wild, happiness sold,
In the arms of laughter, joy displayed,
In a realm where fables never fade.

Flickering Lights of Fireflies

In the dark, a dance begins,
Tiny lights like cheerful sins,
They blink and twirl, a silly show,
Chasing shadows, to and fro.

One caught a bug, said "You can't fly!"
The bug replied, "I'll surely try!"
Together they spun, a comic plight,
Till dawn stole in, with morning light.

A ladybug laughed at their mess,
"You're both ridiculous, I must confess!"
But they just smiled, those glow bugs bright,
Charmed by dreams that lit the night.

So here's to bugs that light the way,
In twinkling hues, they laugh and play,
With giggles shared in magical glow,
Each flicker holds a secret, you know.

A Journey's End in the Grove

Winding paths lead us astray,
With squirrels chattering, in ballet,
A wise old owl, perched up high,
Said, "Buckle up, it's time to fly!"

With every turn, a misstep found,
Tripping over roots, we hit the ground,
A fox cried out, "You're quite the clowns!"
As laughter echoed all around.

The trees sighed deep with a soft grin,
While chipmunks yelled, "Come join the din!"
So we danced with glee, through dappled beams,
Chasing sunlight, chasing dreams.

At journey's end, a feast laid wide,
Pinecone muffins, all piled side by side,
And as we ate, a thought ran clear,
Life's better here, with friends and cheer!

The Soliloquy of Saplings

Little saplings stretching tall,
Whisper secrets, laughing small,
"I saw a leaf jump off today!"
"Where'd it go?" "Oh, far away!"

One dreamed of being a mighty tree,
While others giggled, "Just wait and see!"
A gust of wind, they danced around,
Swaying with joy that made no sound.

The soil grumbled, "Don't grow so fast!"
"Let's enjoy youth, it's a blast!"
With roots entangled, the fun began,
In the shade of the wise old man.

As twilight fell, shadows grew long,
They murmured quietly, still and strong,
"We may be small, but we are free,
In this patch of earth, that's home to me!"

Echoes of Eucalyptus

In the wind, a funny voice,
Whispers echoes, making noise,
"Have you heard the tale of the breeze?"
"It tickles leaves, puts minds at ease!"

Tall and proud, the trees are wise,
One to another, sharing lies,
"I'm the tallest!" one boasts loud,
While clouds above just giggle proud.

The blooms below burst out in cheer,
"Let's play hide and seek, oh dear!"
But bees are buzzing, calling for tea,
"Who joke this time? Come play with me!"

As dusk descends, with laughter bright,
They share stories in fading light,
For in this grove of leafy cheer,
Every moment sparkles here.

Chasing Sunbeams Between the Trees

In the woods, I spy a light,
A squirrel dancing, what a sight!
It jumps and twirls, oh what a tease,
While I trip over knobby knees.

Frogs leap high from watery ponds,
Wearing crowns made of rubber bands.
As I chase the sun's warm glow,
They ribbit jokes and put on a show.

A tree with a tongue, can you believe?
It tastes the wind and moves like a weave.
Whispering secrets of ancient times,
While I gather stories and write silly rhymes.

So join the dance, let's twirl and spin,
In the glimmering light, let laughter begin!
The trees may giggle, the grass will sway,
In this whimsical world, we'll play all day.

Echoing Laughter of the Locust

Locusts chirp their favorite tune,
Making a racket from sun to moon.
They laugh at my flat-footed clumsiness,
While I try to dance with agility and finesse.

A hidden snail with a party hat,
Slimes sticky trails, what of that?
With its friends, the ants do a jig,
While I ponder if I'm too big.

The trees chuckle, a rustic choir,
As I miss my step, my heart caught in fire.
And every tumble turns into glee,
As even the mushrooms giggle at me.

So let's applaud this rambunctious spree,
Nature's jokes are wild and free!
With a hop and a skip, in mirth we dwell,
The locusts chime their happy bell.

Where the Wild Things Wonder

In the glades where shadows play,
Wild things roam by night and day.
A raccoon donned in shades so bright,
Sips soda while the moon takes flight.

A bear juggles berries with flair,
Laughing loud without a care.
He slips and spills a tart surprise,
And honey drips from all his pies.

Squirrel gossip flows like creek streams,
In this land where whimsy beams.
Every critter wears a smile,
While sharing tales that stretch a mile.

So venture where the stories blend,
Where mischief and fun will never end.
With a hop and wiggle, join the throng,
In the wonderland we all belong.

Twilight's Embrace in Nature's Hold

As daylight fades, the fireflies gleam,
Whispers flutter in the twilight dream.
An owl in glasses reads a book,
While I'm lost in a magical nook.

The wind brings giggles through the trees,
Tickling leaves like a cunning tease.
A hedgehog wears a dapper coat,
While we share tales afloat on a boat.

Bats flip-flap, hosting a race,
In a sky filled with stars, we find our place.
Each creature has a joke to tell,
As laughter rings like a cheerful bell.

So gather near as night unfolds,
In nature's arms, let the funny mold.
With each chuckle, we'll glow and glow,
Under the stars in a whimsical show.

Dappled Dreams and Hollow Echoes

In the woods where shadows play,
The squirrels plot their grand ballet.
With acorns flying left and right,
It's a nutty show, what a sight!

The owls hoot in their fancy hats,
Debating who's the best of cats.
While rabbits giggle in a race,
Hopping fast, just to keep pace!

Legends of the Lichen-Laced Path

A raccoon with a silver spoon,
Sipping tea beneath the moon.
He tells tales of late-night snacks,
While foxes scheme with sneaky hacks.

The toads croak in their funky tie,
Encouraging the bees to fly.
They dance in rhythms by the stream,
A lichen party, what a meme!

Soft Footfalls on Ferny Floors

Geranium the sprightly deer,
Wears a crown, she has no fear.
With every step, the ferns all sway,
As she leads the fabled way!

A badger bursts in laughter loud,
Dancing 'neath a leafy shroud.
With silly moves, they spin and twirl,
Nature's stage, a funny whirl!

Songs of the Swaying Branches

The branches sway, they hum a tune,
Beneath the gaze of a grumpy raccoon.
With each rustle, a secret shared,
In leafy whispers, all are bared.

A snail with dreams of being quick,
Challenges a worm to do a trick.
But with a sigh, they both depart,
To laugh and tease, now that's true art!

Murmurs of the Woodland Spirits

In the thicket, giggles wisp,
A squirrel's dance, a playful skip.
Owls wear glasses, quite the sight,
Beneath the moon's soft, silver light.

Frogs in ties sing suave ballads,
While rabbits joke in fearsome salad.
The trees are gossiping with glee,
About the acorns' latest spree.

Luminous fireflies flash their cues,
As hedgehogs share their gossip news.
A fox with flair, a charming grin,
Mocks the snail who just can't win.

So wander here, where whimsy reigns,
And laughter echoes in the lanes.
Nature's tales, both strange and sweet,
Invite you to join this laughter suite.

The Tapestry of Twigs

A tapestry where twigs entwine,
Each knot a story, sweet and fine.
A chattering bird with quite the hat,
Tells of a cow who thinks she's a cat.

The chipmunk juggles acorns round,
While badgers twirl, with grace unbound.
The mushrooms giggle, knit in caps,
As hedges hide from napping laps.

Crafty raccoons clip coupons rare,
For berries that bloom beyond compare.
In this grand weave of leafy cheer,
One must simply laugh while near.

So let the twigs tell tales anew,
Of mischief, laughter—the forest brew.
Join in the fun, don't be shy,
Nature's humor will surely fly.

Whimsy Among the Willow Wisps

Beneath the wisps where willows wave,
A dancing breeze the branches brave.
A shadowy fox in a tutu spins,
While the elves plot tricks with goofy grins.

Butterflies gossip, high in the air,
About the beetle's dapper hair.
Crickets chirp in funny rhymes,
To keep the squirrels guessing their crimes.

The fish in ponds wear tiny hats,
Debating over the best of chats.
While frogs play leapfrog, round and round,
With each great splash, laughter's found.

Amidst the whispers of soft sage,
Joyful tales leap from every page.
Join in the fun, without a fuss,
In this world of whimsy, what's not to trust?

Starlit Canopy Chronicles

Under the stars, the tales unfold,
A nightingale sings of the brave and bold.
Mice in armor, with cheese for shields,
March into battle, their fate revealed.

The owls survey with knowing eyes,
As crickets tune to the moonlit skies.
The playful winds weave stories dear,
Of dancing shadows and warmest cheer.

Raccoons host feasts with snacks galore,
While hedgehogs play the drums and snore.
The trends of the night are quite absurd,
As each creature prances, singing their word.

So lay beneath this twinkling scene,
And marvel at what has never been.
For night brings laughter, wild and free,
In this canopy's vast tapestry.

Whispers of the Woodlands

In the woods where squirrels play,
And sing their songs all day,
A rabbit hops, a raccoon sighs,
While owls debate in moonlit skies.

Mice wear hats, they dance and twirl,
As tiny ants start to unfurl,
A dance-off on the forest floor,
Who knew they could shake it more?

The pines gossip, their needles shake,
While a wise old turtle makes a cake,
The type of treat that's hard to find,
A berry smash that's quite divine!

A cloud of butterflies takes flight,
Chasing shadows, oh what a sight,
They giggle and glide just like a dream,
In this woodlands' wild, whimsical scheme.

Echoes Beneath the Canopy

Beetles march in stiff parade,
While tree trunks wear a leafy shade,
An acorn slipped, a merry thud,
And frogs jump high in joyful floods.

Squirrels sell their nutty wares,
While trees whisper secret flares,
A hapless fox slips on a log,
And claims it's just an old toad's fog!

The brook gurgles jokes, quite absurd,
While chatty birds share every word,
A pie made from the ripest fruits,
Served in hats made of snazzy boots!

The shadows giggle, the sunlight beams,
Nature's got some zany schemes,
In this wild spot, with laugh and cheer,
Life's a comedy when you're out here!

A Tapestry of Twisted Roots

Roots that twist like silly bands,
Play hide and seek beneath the sands,
A porcupine spins tales of yore,
While rabbits knock on leafy doors.

The deer put on a funny show,
With synchronized hops in a row,
While chipmunks join the tap-dance craze,
Filling the woods with laughter and praise.

A wise old badger claims the stage,
With jokes that surely could engage,
Each critter rolling, laughing loud,
Gathered round in a joyful crowd!

The sunlight catches, each laugh a glow,
With nature's jesters putting on a show,
Life's a riot amidst all the trees,
Where giggles spread like the summer breeze.

Secrets in the Shade

In the shade, gnomes hide in play,
Juggling mushrooms day by day,
A sneaky fox in oversized shoes,
Dances silly to the forest blues.

The owls hoot in quirky tones,
While lizards skate on ancient stones,
An echo of laughter fills the air,
As hedgehogs spin on a wild dare!

A boastful crow with dazzling flair,
Tells of a dance-off that's beyond compare,
As the moon winks with a little jest,
It's a nightly show, the very best!

With giggles swirling 'round each tree,
This secret spot is wild and free,
In nature's heart, the laughter plays,
Where every shade holds funny ways.

The Labyrinth of Leafy Dreams

In the maze of green, I roam wide,
Finding squirrels who seem to hide.
They chitter and chatter, scampering quick,
With acorns they juggle, a nutty trick.

A rabbit hops past, a top hat askew,
"Is this a party? I came for the brew!"
His whiskers twitch with a comical flair,
As he slips on a leaf, unaware of the scare.

The sunbeams giggle, as shadows play,
With whispers of antics throughout the day.
The plants gossip low; what could they tell?
If only I knew, I'd chuckle as well!

But paths intertwine, round and round,
Where surprises await in the shimmering ground.
Each twist reveals oddities, jokes in a bunch,
In this leafy realm, laughter's the punch!

Secrets in the Shade

Underneath leaves, whispers roam,
Like mischief-makers far from home.
A frog in a crown, singing the blues,
While crickets do tap-dance in their shoes.

The wise old owl hoots with delight,
"Watch out, dear cat, it's a game of fright!"
Yet the cat just yawns, not one bit fazed,
Dozing amidst the jokes that were raised.

A turtle slow-waltzes, oh what a sight,
While fireflies flicker, put up a light.
"Can't catch me!" giggles the breeze as it sweeps,
Laughter erupts from the roots and the leaves.

In chambers of green where the sunlight drips,
Every corner holds laughter, each leaf does do flips.
So come gather 'round for the show of the day,
With secrets and smiles to light up your way!

The Timeless Thrum of the Thicket

In the thicket so thick where the tall tales bloom,
Nibbling gnomes scatter, making room.
A hedgehog in boots attempts to dance,
Tripping on roots, oh what a chance!

Mice plan a feast, a picnic on grass,
While the butterflies flutter, hoping to pass.
"Is there cake?" squeaks a chipmunk with glee,
As he tries to scale a very tall tree.

Beneath the grand branches where secrets are spun,
Squirrels tell stories, each one just for fun.
The murmur of mischief flows like a stream,
In this lively thicket, it's all a big dream!

So listen closely to the rhythm of leaves,
Where mirth and humor play tricks on deceives.
And though time may pass among laughter and cheer,
Each moment together draws friends ever near!

A Treetop Tale Unfolds

High above ground where the breezes collide,
A squirrel named Chip takes a bouncy ride.
On branches he leaps, with a flick of his tail,
While birds crack up, reading his mail.

A tale comes alive in the canopy's light,
Where shadows grow bigger, stretching in fright.
A mouse with a mustache, declaring a feast,
Wants cheese on a platter, not crumbs from a beast!

The owl gives a hoot, sounding quite wise,
"Join in the fun! No need for disguise!"
But the bunnies are busy plotting a game,
Of hide and seek, oh what a name!

So up in the branches, the stories will swing,
With laughter that echoes, oh what joy they bring.
For nature's a stage, and we're all the stars,
We giggle and dance beneath the moonlight's bars!

Starlit Paths and Moonlit Dreams

Under the glow of a cheeky star,
Squirrels dance with their acorn jar,
They twirl and spin, a comical sight,
Making shadows that giggle at night.

Mice hold a party, cheese on a plate,
Crickets debate if they're early or late,
The owl rolls his eyes, quite bored of the show,
While fireflies flicker like stars down below.

The raccoon with a mask starts a funny bit,
Imitating humans—oh, wasn't it lit!
The breeze whispers secrets, tickling the trees,
As laughter echoes with every soft breeze.

Then morning arrives, they all scurry back,
To hide in the roots, and resume their snack,
With dreams of the night still bright in their heads,
They snooze till the moon, then off to mischief, they tread.

Journey Through the Verdant Veil

Past blooms that giggle, and branches that sway,
A tortoise tells jokes while he lags on his way,
"Why did the beetle cross over the path?
To roll on a log, and escape the giraffe!"

The hedgehog dressed smart with a tie and a hat,
Proclaims through a laugh, "No hair! How's about that?"
While butterflies snicker, in colorful flight,
"They might have nice clothes but can't win a fight!"

Beneath leafy arches, they run and they play,
A badger named Bob leads the scuffle today,
He slips on a leaf, and what a surprise!
The sunlight bursts through, making shadows arise.

Together they tumble, collide, and then rise,
With laughter contagious, like worms in disguise,
In this splendid wonder, they act without care,
As nature takes notes, giving smiles everywhere.

Tales of Treetops and Time

A toucan recounts exaggerated tales,
Of grand, grandmothers who powered their sails,
With branches for oars and leaves for a map,
They sighed with adventure, and laughed through the gap.

The woodpecker chuckles, "Oh such a grand feat,
But who'll clean the mess when they all take a seat?"
As laughter erupts from the shrubbery grey,
While worms hold their sides in a delightful display.

The wind whispers jokes and the leaves chime in tune,
A raccoon with flair is plotting a boon,
"Let's dress up the owls in fashions so bright,
And host a grand ball under starry delight!"

As night drifts in slowly, the stories grow bold,
While guardians of giggles look on as foretold,
These antics remind us, under starlit designs,
The joy of our laughter in nature aligns.

Heartstrings Tied to Nature's Rhythm

Along the pathway where wildflowers grow,
A frog in a top hat sings songs by the flow,
"Chirp, chirp!" the crickets add beat to the tune,
With echoes of laughter that rise to the moon.

Amidst the bright blooms, a fox tells a jest,
While a snail on a leaf takes a leisurely rest,
"Have you heard of the chicken who danced in the rain?
She slipped on a puddle and shrieked with disdain!"

So on goes the party, each creature so bold,
With tales of the night getting merrily told,
As creatures all play, their hearts full of cheer,
Engaging in magic, while nature draws near.

And when the sun rises, the laughter will fade,
But stories remain in the memories made,
Before they retreat to their nooks and their nooks,
They vow to return for the next day's funny books.

Stolen Moments Among the Trees

Squirrels plan their grand parade,
Nuts in hand, their raucous charade.
While rabbits in capes take flight with glee,
Chasing shadows, wild and free.

Branches wiggle, leaves whisper low,
Dancing secrets that only they know.
A hiccup from a chipmunk brings a cheer,
As laughter rings in the crisp, cool air.

Mushrooms chuckle in tattered suits,
Complaining 'bout uninvited roots.
As flowers wear their best bloom,
Swapping tales of gloom and gloom.

In these moments, time just slips,
Frogs in bow ties, they do their flips.
With giggles echoing around the bend,
Nature's joy, a never-ending friend.

A Ballad for the Burgeoning

In jest, the bushes start to sway,
As fledgling sprouts join the play.
Butterflies laugh, their wings a blur,
Giving a wink to the shy panther.

The old tree croaks a joke so dry,
Said a bird, 'Only the squirrels fly!'
Hiccups bubble in the mossy bed,
While critters gather 'round, well-fed.

A snail wearing shades takes a slow stroll,
Deeming himself the rock 'n' roll soul.
Buzzy bees duet in the air,
With humor blooming everywhere.

Thus sings the life in the thriving din,
Of cheeky roots that know they can win.
To frolic on a sunny beam,
With a giggling brook as the theme.

Beneath the Boughs of Breezes

Beneath the boughs, a cozy nook,
Where giggling ferns come out to look.
A hedgehog spins his tales of fright,
While ants hold court in the moon's soft light.

A breeze sneezes, oh what a gasp!
Leaves tumble down in a playful clasp.
Woodpeckers dance on old tree trunks,
As critters giggle, shaking off shrinks.

A wily fox flips over a log,
Trying hard to catch a dialogue.
As mushrooms tease with their twinkling hints,
Complaining 'bout unsightly mints.

Together they sing, under twilight's sway,
Charmed by chants of the woodland play.
Each rustle a laugh, a gentle shout,
As night's curtain falls, all chuckles out.

Solstice Dreams in the Green

In the green where dreams collide,
A raccoon wears a crown with pride.
He juggles acorns, not a care,
While owls giggle from their lair.

Sunbeams tickle the underbrush,
In a world where no one's in a rush.
Lizards debate in their tiny tongues,
About the songs that the elder sung.

From every nook, laughter spills,
As playful squirrels hide their thrills.
Fireflies sketch with luminescent dreams,
Juvenile artists with glowing beams.

With each new joke floating in air,
The earth spins in joy, debonair.
For in these woods, life's not too keen,
When nature laughs, all's evergreen.

Glimmers in the Green Abyss

In the woods where the squirrels dance,
A raccoon steals a glance,
He thinks he's a human, you see,
With a snack in his paw, full of glee.

The trees whisper secrets in wind's gentle sigh,
While ants stand tall, waving goodbye.
A fox gives a wink, she's on a grand quest,
Hunting for truffles, but cheese is her best!

Mushrooms giggle, popping from soil,
In a party of fungi, they twist and toil.
With hats of all colors, they sway to the beat,
Creating a ruckus, a fungus retreat!

As the sun dips low, shadows do play,
A bunny hops clumsily, loses his way.
With a chuckle and jump, he finds his own crew,
In the heart of the woods, the silliness grew.

The Spirit of Sedge and Sun

Beneath the bright rays, the patchwork unfolds,
Where tales of the wild, in jest, are retold.
A turtle in shades, with a grin on his face,
He's slow but he's savvy, an ace in the race!

A butterfly flutters, with mischief in flight,
Chasing a beetle who thinks he's so bright.
They spin and they twirl through petals of cheer,
In a dance of delight, no worries, no fear!

The crickets compose, a symphony grand,
While a snail in a shell plays a wizard's hand.
He conjures up magic with each little slide,
In a world where the oddities can only reside!

As evening descends and the lantern bugs glow,
A hedgehog in jackets steals the main show.
With laughter and joy, they party till night,
In the realm of the quirky, everything's right!

Chronicles of the Canopied Cure

In the shade of the branches, where giggles emerge,
A wise old owl gives raccoons a surge.
"Why not try juggling? You give it a go!"
They drop all their snacks, oh the splats and the show!

A squirrel in boots thinks he's ready to brawl,
He challenges trees, but they only stand tall.
With acorns as armor, he takes a grand swing,
Yet all that he hits is a sweet, chirpy thing.

A playful breeze whispers tales of the day,
While grasshoppers giggle, trying to play.
With dance-offs and prances, they clamor for fun,
In the game of the silly, they forever will run!

As dusk casts its charm and the stars start to peek,
A glowworm arrives with a glimmering cheek.
"Who's ready for karaoke?" she sings with a beam,
And all of the critters join in the dream!

A Journey Through Verdant Vows

On a path lined with laughter, the creatures can roam,
A rabbit named Benny has lost his way home.
With maps made of leaves, he searches for signs,
While a chipmunk shouts, "Come, join in the fun times!"

A ladybug patterns her wings with delight,
Watching ants march parade in a march left and right.
"Is that a snail's shell or a cozy little den?"
"No, it's just his new hat—fashion's back again!"

Under canopies woven of trunks and of tales,
A weasel dressed sharp, he delivers the mails.
He trips on a vine and lands slick on a log,
Puffing and huffing, "Oops! A bit of a smog!"

In the heart of this realm, where nothing seems gray,
The creatures sing songs, a cacophony play.
Their laughter and joy echo wide and profound,
In a symphony silly, the quirkiest sound!

The Wish of the Whispering Pines

In the groove of the trees, they chuckle and sway,
Pines wish for a breeze, to frolic and play.
They toss out their needles, a prickly surprise,
While raccoons plan parties, under moonlit skies.

Squirrels wear hats made of acorns and fluff,
They dance in the branches, all clever and tough.
A rabbit insists that he's quite the best chef,
And serves up his carrots with flair, no less!

The owl with his spectacles watches the show,
Laughing at antics of friends down below.
With winks and with hoots, he joins in the fun,
As shadows grow long, it's a bash 'til they're done.

In the nook of the grove, they finish the night,
Grateful for giggles and birthday cake bites.
The whispering pines, they know the right prance,
In their woodsy retreat, there's always a chance!

Reverie on Roots and Reeds

Along the stream, reeds bob like a band,
Swaying together, they make quite a stand.
A frog in a beret croaks tales of delight,
While bugs with their ties bring laughs to the night.

Roots wear their jackets, all knotted and neat,
Making shoes for the critters, oh what a feat!
They trip over twigs while they waltz in the glow,
As the moon joins the bash, putting on quite the show.

Tadpoles in tuxedos dive deep just to play,
They bounce and they leap in a froggy ballet.
Giggling willows offer shade for the crowd,
As the laughter grows loud, and the night feels proud.

With each rippling wave, a giggle will flow,
In this reverie land, all worries let go.
Roots and reeds mingle, with sprouts that dance free,
In their playful kingdom, where joy's key to be!

Twilight Tints the Thicket

As twilight descends, hues dance in the air,
A chameleon jigs, slick moves without care.
Beneath blooming blooms, the shadows reappear,
While fireflies twinkle, bringing laughter and cheer.

The hedgehog in boots slides, skidding with glee,
A badger in specs hums a jig with the bees.
All creatures unite in their evening parade,
With twirls, dips, and spins, not a moment delayed.

Crickets compose a song, lively and bold,
As the owl conducts, sharing wisdom untold.
They tap, they stomp, on the dirt without shame,
A tangled-up mass, yet they all know the game.

With a flip and a flap, the night off they go,
In a joyful fiesta, with hearts all aglow.
Twilight, a blessing, for every small beast,
Where laughter and rhythm never cease in their feast!

Beneath the Bough: A Yarn

Beneath the grand bough, a tale starts to weave,
Of critters that gather and joys they conceive.
A raccoon tells stories, each sillier still,
Of treasure-filled eggs that are guarded by quills.

A wise old turtle, slow with his grin,
Adds laughter to tales of the mess he's been in.
He tripped on a root while dancing with ease,
And landed headfirst in a patch of tall cheese.

The laughter erupts, as owls hoot in glee,
As the raccoon, quite proud, brings forth eggplant tea.
With tea cups from leaves, they sip and they chat,
While a gopher digs holes to lean back and nap.

As dusk claims the sky, their stories spread wide,
What magic unfurls, with friends by your side!
Beneath the grand bough, all worries take flight,
In a land filled with joy, from morning till night!

The Language of Moss and Stone

Moss whispers secrets, soft and green,
Stones giggle lightly, a sight unseen.
Trees shake their branches, a dance so sweet,
Creatures hide chuckling, quick on their feet.

Squirrels debate on the best nut stash,
While owls hoot loudly, giving a splash.
In this grand talk, the ferns roll their eyes,
As dandelions puff out witty sighs.

Rabbits plot mischief, a playful scheme,
While snails take their time, slow as a dream.
The sun tickles leaves, laughter unbound,
Nature's own humor, in whispers profound.

So next time you wander, take a good listen,
To the chatter and chuckles, don't you dare miss them!
Every twig, every bark, has a joke or a tale,
In this lively realm where giggles prevail.

Enchanted Glades and Gentle Breezes

In glades where the laughter of breezes collide,
Daisies do pirouettes, with petals spread wide.
Here, the robins belt out their silly tunes,
While gathering twigs to craft hats like cartoons.

A fox with a flair sports a bright feather,
Pretending he's king, in this light breezy weather.
The butterflies waltz in the bright afternoon,
While grasshoppers croon a fun, silly tune.

The trickster raccoons raid the picnic baskets,
With snacks for their parties, they plot their vast tasks.
Chasing their tails, they tumble with glee,
In this madcap glade where all wish to be.

With laughter's sweet echo, joy fills the air,
In a tapestry woven with giggles to share.
Each breeze carries laughter, a wondrous decree,
In enchanted meadows, where spirits run free.

Murmurs of the Ancient Grove

In the ancient grove, where shadows debate,
Branches gossip softly about the next fate.
Acorns create plots, in a council of sorts,
As critters gather round for their whispered reports.

The owls tell tales of the moon's funny dance,
While rabbits roll dice, hoping for chance.
Old trees chuckle 'bout times that were bold,
Their bark-shaped smiles and roots turning gold.

A porcupine jests, 'Don't prick up your skin!'
As the wise old crow caws, 'Let the fun begin!'
Mice scamper in circles, while snickers abound,
In this lively refuge where laughter is found.

So join in the murmurs, don't be shy or coy,
The grove's filled with humor and abundant joy.
Every rustle of leaves says, 'Come share a jest!'
In this playful place, where all are the best.

Sylvan Serenade at Dusk

As dusk drapes the woods in a shimmery glow,
Crickets strike up a tune, a lively show.
Fireflies twinkle like stars in a snare,
Winking and blinking with a whimsical flair.

The trees sway gently, their branches swish,
While frogs take the stage, croaking their wish.
'Bring on the moon!' bellows a bold bear,
As a chorus of owls joins in the air.

Bunnies in bow ties start a dance-off spree,
While raccoons cheer loudly, hyping the glee.
Under the twilight, in laughter they bask,
As the magical night plays its jester-like task.

So listen intently, as night softly sings,
In sylvan serenades, where mirth always clings.
With giggles and chirps, let your heart flutter,
In nature's sweet song, where joy is no utter.

Dance of the Dappled Deer

In the clearing, hooves take flight,
Dancing wildly in the light.
With a leap and twist, they prance,
Chasing shadows in a dance.

Squirrels giggle from the trees,
As they rustle in the breeze.
A rabbit joins, with ears so tall,
Together they all have a ball!

Oh, the fun, oh, the laughter,
A tale of woodland happily ever after.
With a wink and a silly spin,
Even the tiniest bugs join in!

But oops! A misstep leads to tumble,
As the deer land in a fumble.
With a grin and a shuffle out,
They bounce back, leaping about!

Shadows of the Sunlit Grove

In the grove where shadows play,
Squirrels chatter through the day.
Sunbeams dance upon the ground,
While giggles echo all around.

A raccoon dons a funny hat,
Parading like a silly cat.
With mischief in his twinkling eyes,
He sneaks off with a sweet surprise!

Leaves whisper secrets, oh so bright,
As they sway with pure delight.
The birds join in a merry song,
Announcing that the fun is strong!

But watch out for a grumpy bee,
Who buzzes by all full of glee.
He thinks he's king, can't miss his chance,
To join the joyful, buzzing dance!

The Silent Language of Leaves

Rustling leaves with whispers sweet,
Converse in rhythms, oh so neat.
A wind's chuckle, a little breezy,
Tickles the trees, it's quite the tease-y!

Owl named Oliver gives a hoot,
Sipping soft dew, dressed in a suit.
With wisdom, he too joins the jest,
Laughs softly, thinking he knows best.

Mice have formed a clever band,
Holding tiny paws, they take a stand.
In a conga line, they slide and sway,
Knocking acorns, making play!

But beware the sudden slap!
A branch drops down with a little clap.
The laughter stops; all eyes look round,
To see who lost the acorn crown!

Bark-Bound Dreams

In a treehouse made of dreams,
Squirrels plot with silly schemes.
With acorn hats and gowns of bark,
They laugh and play from dawn till dark.

A wise old turtle drags his shell,
Thinking how to spin a tale so well.
He blinks slowly, then proposes fun,
A treasure hunt to be quickly done!

With giggles echoing near and far,
They search for things like a shiny star.
A hidden twig, a crumb of cheese,
All treasures found with giggling ease!

But as they leap and race about,
They tumble forward with a shout.
Through the laughter, they share a scream,
Finding joy in their bark-bound dream!

www.ingramcontent.com/pod-product-compliance
Lightning Source LLC
Chambersburg PA
CBHW071828160426
43209CB00003B/233